The Chain Coral Chorus:
A Geopoetic Waybook

R. M. Francis

Published by Playdead Press

© R. M. Francis 2023

R. M. Francis has asserted his rights under the Copyright, Design and Patents Act, 1988, to be identified as the author of this work.

A CIP catalogue record for this book is available from the British Library.

ISBN 978-1-915533-10-4

Playdead Press
www.playdeadpress.com

For Lee Prescott

1.

What is the Chain Coral Chorus?

In July 2020 I became Poet in Residence for the Black Country Geological Society (BCGS). A role enabled by the University of Wolverhampton Doctoral College's Early Research Award Scheme.

I explored the sites that make up the UNESCO Black Country Geopark – writing a series of poems inspired by and set in these wonderful places. The poems in this collection are creative responses to the environment, asking how the geological make-up of the land impacts, connects and clashes with the overlooked cultures of the region. This work has been enhanced by the important geological research of the BCGS: furthering the messages of geo-conservation and introducing newcomers to geology, poetry and the region's rich history.

The Black Country is famous for its role in the Industrial Revolution. Its industrial heritage forged unique and important communities and cultures; this, in many ways, was connected to the grounds that gave life to these cultures – the fossil and mineral rich grounds dating back to the Silurian era. One such fossil is Chain Coral; a now extinct form of colonising coral. Single cells branch off, forming helix, webs or chain patterns. This species colonised the area that was to become known as the Black Country. These fossil-chained grounds gave rise to the chainmakers, steelers and miners – the chain continues to be an important symbol of the region's heritage, representing strong communal / cultural links. Chains run deep in the region's cultural psyche – they run deep in the deep time soils.

These poems re-figure our relationship with the local environment; both in its surfaces and depths, the building materials and the forces that create them. This project considers these issues in an overlooked region, famed for its 'dark satanic mills', in conjunction with conservation, ecology, sustainability, and new ways of experiencing place in the Anthropocene.

Wyvern

There's patterns to the bell pits, ay there. Chain links from
chain coral's infinite coda. Traverse their cusps. Breathe slow.
Tek quiet steps. In this cycle yo'll spy the slow breath an'
quiet steps 'a strange patterns. Then consider not what yo' see,
but what is seeing yo'. As yo' tred it treds into yo'.

If yo' know where to look, it ay just a woodland, iss a gateway
wheya things stretch out an' loop, ay it?! Loops an' fractals in
honeycomb revenants – chain coral's infinite coda. They used
to come 'ere, but they doh come' ere no more.

When birch, oak and elm took back the slag 'a pit bonk an'
quarry, they wove wild roots round the wyvern. It still
stretches from time to time an' still kips travellers to paths.
Even non-believers follow known routes, half-knowing what
sleepin' beasts am under foot.

Thicket thresholds divide Cooper's Bonk an' Snetter estates.
They used to come ere but they doh come ere no more. No
more prayer at 'alf-cut pyramids, drilled wi' rusted rods. Just
hush an' hushing. The almost silent hush from chain coral's
infinite coda. A wyvern breathes.

In the edges, hedge gives way between disused railway line an'
wheat saplings, an' teen-oaks part branches. They used to
come ere but they doh come ere no more. These doorless
thresholds am no go zones, but for fleeting flesh scrumpers.
Behind ruined cluniac bricks. Between municipal toilet an'
playground – still, silent, sedated. Crepuscular rays find ways

through thicket, draw yo' away from path for a second, yo'
thought yo' caught the glimpse of wyvern entering / re-
entering, day yo'. A moment moves into Alice-Time.
Some paths ay med for mon. Some ay med by mon. We scaled
em anyroad, day we? Up an height on the Wrenna, ower
shadows ovver ower streets, stems an' stone. They used to
come 'ere but they doh come 'ere no more.

Fossil Pizza

Down Daw End
and the damp dank
of moss-licked blue bricks
arched above the thunder-clack
currents of daily commuters,
we circle into reef patches of first life:

shell-Brittlestar-sponge
    I
    V
cephAlopod
  aLgae
  V
  Eurypterid
     u
     g
   horn
  cooksonia
    e

Cartilage, vascular tissue
and movement
held in white world
of stilly soils.

Bibble

She said, *iss just a rock,*
and she was right. *Yo'm*
right, me wench,
an' thass the rub,
iss just a rock.
And they were just
the sum of each.

Petrologic Cinquain .1

Mica,
craton bedded
in pegmatite jigsaw.
Desquamate for kirazuri:
Glittered.

Through Filth

Attend!
Descend wi' me, mucker,
down below grounds
'a Paganel's priory, 'ere 'ides
the rhizome-echo 'a cluniac
monks an' theya prayer
enkindled, enflamed, like
our own Smithys scorched
core to gem, sand to glass,
dust to daggers, smelt
by quicksilver fingers 'a
nailmekkin' kins full 'a ken
for our caverns. These caverns.
Descend wi' me, mucker.
Descend down below wrenna
roots an' lime where the cut
chainlinks nidhogg, yggdrasil
to cornershop, callcentre,
from chain-coral helixing
revelations to brackets
'a battle, ghost-ship, colony –
empires am iverin' an' overin' 'ere,
sendin' out cantin' whisps
'a caggy-'eaded scrappies
older than god-time.

Attend!
Moist ore moves
in slow spit splitting fermi –
firm as fossil, cold

12

as core – there ay a Svedberg
of scuttles in 'ere;
just patient sediments
wi' the brood 'a halysite
silica shale, tracks
'a tabulate ordering roots
for protobeings an' protoaction.
Down 'ere weem
the stone an' slick sand
fertilities for steeler, glassmekker,
almost-teen lad wi' ommer,
wi' chissel, wi' lens to spy
crinoid ruins - insects set
in geonest. Attend! 'Ere rests
the Dudley Bug. Moloch. Iss ower
slow burn municipal crest –
elytra protects brave chests
in protean soils an' lets us swarm:
in stercore invenitur.

2.

Towards a Black Country Geopoetics

GEO = *Earth, Soil, Ground*

POETICS = *To make. The process of making*

Geopoetics is a philosophy or way of being which puts the Earth at the centre of experience and perception. It reconnects us with the natural realms and aims to express this grounded sense of self in earthness itself. For Kenneth White it is concerned with "a disengaging of the mind from rationalism, realism and materialism, and an openness to direct apprehension". Geopoetic ways of being, seeing and thinking are drawn from sensory, bodily and instinctual knowledge and focus on the ways these lead us to the sacred and / or transformative. White calls it the enormous:

> The geopoeticist is immediately placed in the enormous. I mean this first in the quantitative, encyclopaedic sense (I am not against the quantitative, provided that the force is able to support it), then, in the sense of the exceptional, of e-norm (outside the standards). By conveying a great deal of matter, of terrestrial matter, with a broad sense of things and of being, geopoetics opens up a space of culture, thought, life. In short, a world [...] It's not just

about scholarship and history, it's about tracing a geography of the mind.[1]

Fellow Geopoet and Critic, Tony McManus puts it this way:

> If White's sense of alienation is both intellectual and existential, the intellectual nomadism which explores ways beyond the alienation consists of intellectual enquiry – reading and writing, the cultivation of the mind – but also existential experience – errance and residence, the cultivation of the body and the senses [...] The socio-personal identity is lost and one experiences an 'enlargening of identity.[2]

Olivier Delbard defines it as: "A mental geography [...] where the physical intuition and mental intellectual insights interconnect, in the open world".[3] This cognitive awareness is focused on experiences and perceptions of the earth, and with our sense of self in that context. We do this through acute awareness of our surroundings, by touching the earth and through attempts to awaken the multitudinous ways of thinking and perceiving. It is, White argues, "an awareness of

---

[1] White, K., 'The Great Field of Geopoetics' from *The International Institute of Geopoetics: Founding Texts, https://www.institut-geopoetique.org/fr/textes-fondateurs/8-le-grand-champ-de-la-geopoetique*

[2] McManus, T., 'Kenneth White: A Transcendental Scott' from *Grounding a World: Essays on the Work of Kenneth White*, eds Bowd, G., Forsdick, C., Bissell, N., (Alba Editions: 2005) pp.14-16

[3] Delbard, O., 'Walking the Edge: Kenneth White's Landscape-Mindscape' from *Grounding a World: Essays on the Work of Kenneth White*, eds Bowd, G., Forsdick, C., Bissell, N., (Alba Editions: 2005)

the atmosphere in which we try, without adequate awareness, to live. We would have to go beyond the notion of simply quantitative information, towards the notion of *exformation* (direct encounter with the outside), via *enformation* qualitative".[4] Thinking, White says, "is neither a thread stretched between a subject and an object, nor a revolution of one around the other. Rather, thinking is done in the relationship between territory and land".[5]

Alyson Hallet considers how we might reconnect through a bodily or embodied wisdom:

> I need to talk about the body as a site of intelligence, the body as a place, an environment, a landscape. The body as a wilderness, a wild place, a tamed place, a known and unknown place. A place where relationships are always evolving and changing, where there is a fixed and fragile frame known as skeleton. The body as a site of distress, of memory, of perception. The body as a position, a place of witness and action. The body as beginning and end, receptive and active, the body as transmitter and receiver, as a place where everything happens. The body is our home, our host, the first house of being. This body, my

---

[4] White, K., 'Elements of Geopoetics' from *The International Institute of Geopoetics: Founding Texts, https://www.institut-geopoetique.org/fr/textes-fondateurs/61-elements-de-geopoetique*

[5] White, K., 'A Philosophical Approach to Geopoetics from *The International Institute of Geopoetics: Founding Texts, https://www.institut-geopoetique.org/fr/textes-fondateurs/20-une-approche-philosophique-de-la-geopoetique*

body, born from my mother' body and which contain minerals and elements of the bigger body, the earth, carbon, calcium, titanium.[6]

The brain thinks in terms of territories: maps, diagrams, back-forth and up-down. We understand ourselves and communities in relationship to our known and unknown environments. I believe the ontology of awareness and consciousness is somewhere within the interactions between landscapes (Objects and Movement) Perception (the senses) and thought. Or as White puts it "Knowledge is linked to being, being is linked to the environment, and this complex field can be the site of transcendence".[7]

Geopoetic transcendence is an attempt to understand ourselves, our cultures and communities in relationship to the Anthropocene - a time where we've shaped the earth more than in any other era, and are simultaneously divorced from it. This geopoetic cognitive awakening and world grounding is about "an attitude towards the world which, far from any egoic sentimentalism as from any literary formalism, indissolubly conjoins knowledge and love, knowledge and flavor, logos and

[6] Hallett, A., *Stone Talks* (Axminster: Triarchy Press, 2019) p.67

[7] White, K., 'Humbolt's Geopoetic Peregrinations' from *The International Insitute of Geopoetics: Founding Texts*, *https://www.institut-geopoetique.org/fr/cahiers-de-geopoetique/27-les-peregrinations-geopoetiques-de-humboldt*

eros. A logical erotic sense of the earth!"[8] Don McKay, adds to this saying, "the name Anthropocene, paradoxically enough, puts a crimp in this anthropocentrism ... Inhabiting deep time imaginatively, we give up mastery and gain mutuality".[9] Hawkins agrees, placing more focus on the geological: 'that era in which humans have left a mark on the geological record, has intensified the practical, linguistic, and intellectual rapprochement between arts and sciences, not least around geology.[10] Our awareness of the troubles caused to the non-human by the human, as well the often beautiful collaborations between organic and manmade, subverts anthropocentrism and pulls us into a geo-alertness.

---

[8] Amar, G., 'The Meaning of the Earth' from *The International Institute of Geopoetics:Geopoetic Notebooks, https://www.institut-geopoetique.org/fr/cahiers-de-geopoetique/24-le-sens-de-la-terre*

[9] McKay, Don. "Ediacaran and the Anthropocene: Poetry as a Reader of Deep Time." *GeologicNow.com*, Punctum Books, 4 Dec. 2012, *http://www.geologicnow.com/4_McKay.php*

[10] Hawkins, H, 'Preface' to *Geopoetics in Practice* (New York: Routledge, 2020) xii

3.

Geopoetic practice uses writing practices that draw on geological method and language, and considers human life, culture and society in a deep time context. McKay referred to it as "the place where materialism and mysticism, those ancient enemies, finally come together, have a conversation in which each hearkens to the other, then go out for a drink".[11] In this way, the poet's notebook and the geologist's field journal fuse. This is about deeply connecting to the land and its primal histories and considering ourselves in the context of its deep time; finding new ways of meditating on and communicating about place – who we are, where we're arriving at and from, what building materials give us life and meaning. Linda Russo agrees, saying 'Geopoetics is an attentive remaking, a way of moving forward while locating and digging down into the past'.[12] This follows T. S. Eliot's thoughts in 'Tradition and the Individual Talent' where he discusses the idea of thematic, poetic and language conjugations – disparate elements are brought together in the poem to create something new and larger than the sum of its parts. Eliot describes this process as 'a receptacle for seizing and staring up numberless feelings,

---

[11] McKay, D. *The Shell of the Tortoise* (Kentville: Gaspereau Press: 2011) p.10

[12] Russo, L, 'Introduction' from *Geopoetics in Practice* (New York: Routledge, 2020) 4

phrases, images, which remain there until all the particles can unite to form a new compound'.[13] These numberless things crystallize into new models of expression, becoming 'a concentration, and a new thing resulting from the concentration, of a very great number of experiences'.[14] McKay's conjugation is worded in this way: "Geopoetry makes it legitimate for the natural historian or scientist to speculate and gawk, and equally legitimate for the poet to benefit from close observation, and from some of the amazing facts that science turns up".[15] The melting together of everyday observation and language with scientific method and vernaculars, reaches for new and more geo-focused modes of expressing the Earth and our place in it.

Eco poet, Derek Sheffield, notes the connections between ecology and poetry, suggesting that the notebook becomes a field journal. He says we have "Adam's task – thinking of the right name for a thing".[16] In naming them, we give them spirit

---

[13] Eliot, T.S., 'Tradition and The Individual Talent', in *Perspecta*, Vol.19 (1982), URL: *www.jstor.org/discover/10.2307/1567048?uid=3738032&uid=2129&uid=2&uid=70&uid=4&sid=21103865728181* [Accessed 16/06/16]

[14] ibid

[15] McKay, Don. "Ediacaran and the Anthropocene: Poetry as a Reader of Deep Time".

[16] Sheffield, D., *Geopoetics (Regional Ecology and Poetics)* Conference paper at Cascadia Poetry Festival 2014 https://www.youtube.com/watch?v=d3zs05YhZ0k

– epistemological, narrative and poetic spirit. Like Wilde said, "Nothing existed until art invented it". For Sheffield, following the trail in ecology is the same as following the strange impulse and tides of a poem in progress; an intellectual and physical wayfinding. Drafting equates to evolution and development of the scientific method. Here, the poetics of the creative are informed by the language, processes and observations of the Sciences. Through this the poet comes to recognise, in their poetics, a community of sensory data, vernaculars and interrelationships. The same as ecology: a community of species and connecting interactions. And in this, a recognition of connectedness and otherness. We are part of the system, and yet separate - observers. The Other-Connected is as integral to science as it is to poetry. It is the other and the same together. The Other-Connected also mirrors humanity's anthropocentric positions.

These poetics rely on and are drawn from observation of millenia long bonds and gulfs. The French writer, Francis Ponge, discusses this, saying "[Geopoets] sink into the night of logos - until finally they find themselves at the ROOT level, where things and formulations merge".[17] The geopoet, under

---

[17] Ponge, F. *Le Grande Recueil*, quoted by White in
https://www.institut-geopoetique.org/fr/cahiers-de-geopoetique/31-editorial-du-cahier-n-1

deep time influence, sinks into the darkness / murkiness of where meaning-making is produced (logos) and in doing so find themselves in the sublime of the earth and the sublime of existence. Kenneth White wrote, "I had always been of the persuasion that the richest poetics came from contact with the earth, from a plunge into biospheric space, from an attempt to read the lines of the world".[18] Going on to argue that "This can be done in two ways: either by archaeological work on a language, or by an 'exotic' recourse to other languages with different metaphysics, different initial fictions".[19] We're looking for a language mine, a collecting of words and terms that offer these different illuminating potentialities. But there's more at play too. As White posits, it's "a liberation from our conditioned minds. Once outside you let things be, you let go (letting be isn't a psychological context, it's an ontological one), and you retrieve a topological presence".[20] In my work, this presence is achieved through acute Geological or Deep Time observations. This takes us back to Mckay: "[Geopoetry] provides a crossing point, a bridge over the infamous gulf

---

[18] White, K., 'Presentation of the Institute' from *The International Institute of Geopoetics https://www.institut-geopoetique.org/en/presentation-of-the-institute*

[19] White, K., 'Elements of Geopoetics' from *Edinburgh Review 88, 1992*, p.170 *http://www.alastairmcintosh.com/general/resources/2008-Kenneth-White-Geopoetics.pdf*

[20] White, 'Elements' p. 169

separating scientific from poetic frames of mind, a gulf which has not served us well, nor the planet we inhabit with so little reverence or grace".[21]

This is different from ecopoetry, and distinct from other forms of place-writing or place-journalism. It seeks to express the natural charge of the earth and of existence; giving voice to the strange caverns between human and non-human, intellectual and instinctive. As Delbard states, "All this is much more than travel writing, with its multi-level coherence, taking the reader into the open world, towards abstraction, yet firmly grounded in immediate physical reality".[22] Or in Hallett's words, "Jim Carruth calls himself a rural poet. I could go with that. I am not an ecopoet and never have been. Rural is just fine though, a word that's dirtier, more honest".[23] Hallett identifies with pastoral traditions here. One concerned with the natural and with ecological issues, whilst embracing the murkiness between human and non-human. The geo in my geopoetics is undoubtedly geology (a human and logical meaning-making). The attempted translation of a natural charge in my work is

---

[21] McKay, Don. "Ediacaran and the Anthropocene: Poetry as a Reader of Deep Time".

[22] Delbard, 'Walking the Edge' p.53

[23] Hallet, p. 50

always met with the way it clashes and connects with industrial, post-industrial and everyday life.

This is the foundation of the Chain Coral Chorus. Since the Black Country is so richly steeped in geological wonder, and this gave rise to the cultures and communities that succeeded it, I further geopoetry in the unearthing / grounding available on my doorstep.

Walking Woods Alone (during the coronavirus lockdown, March 2020)

Peace: silent
but for life's invertebrate hum
and winged choristers
tut-chirping in their raptored
judgements. Alone,
step spring paths through
desolate grounds that used
to howl with young men's toil
in the shafts, where limestone
endofolds stained with Silurian
tides: eddies each for each –
we go back and we can never go home.
Alone except for viral eyes – gorgan
for the lungs. On the bank that peaks
out to Tipton, Great Bridge, Coseley;
where yam-yams bitch in nailbite lockup
and tick-tock after tick-tock, painful coughing,
the hum and tut-chirp silence breaks
as fox tries to run down rabbit – caught
only in peripheral, like a ghost's sneeze,
just behind the ear. Blessings hide in time
so narrow, so wide. Peace: so full
of almost-emptiness, so tricked in paranoia.

Coalescence

Just spring –
the last leaves
left from autumn's
mulching leak
into pig iron grounds.
Greywacke, Fireclay, Ironstone
sit turbid at Netherton Spa
where dog walkers and rambling clubs
and pinfold teens and locked in pensioners
sense the spectral gravity beneath feet.
It seems to whine at the flytipped waste. It
takes it into itself. And the buds from Bramble,
Damson, wipe rheum from eyes between quickflash
of bluebell, snowdrop. Rheum drips in Dalton caverns
as in weeping elms and human pores:
this land leaves them colloidal. *We suspend.*

Stratigraphic Time

Ground frost
sits shaded before
May Day rays thaw
and we use its silver
shimmer like fishermen
trails, through fence.
Follow Hawthorn nook,
Cowslip cause, iced
pebble mass to Great Barr Fault
where breccia forges god-time
in red rock displacements.

At the Strata Fold
I'm taken between
dimensions to
steaming swamp
forests, flittering
with glitter-bubbles
of squirming
chilopoda. Its curl
speaks the same song
as Braken; chain coral's
infinite coda.

Then home,
now frosts are mellowed
and circuits and circles
and stirrings clasp
everything.

Laminae

They step columnar joints
up Barrow Hill
to cool contrasting
Snetter redbricks,
where lives varve
around sad climates
in estate and gangs,
grandpa to half-baked toddler:
thass true tharris, thass
the snetter sediment, ay it?
They picnic. Look down
at Fenspool flocculations
and between fag tokes,
tastes of nan's pieces,
link hands to watch
their futures
in rhythmite tides.

4.

The Black Country is a liminal place – it is marginal, unmappable and full of off-kilter landscapes. The Black Country is not quite north and not quite south. It's a strange mix of green space and grey space. Much of its culture is based on its industrial past, but this heritage has been ruined, renovated and built over. It sits in the shadow of its more successful brother Birmingham – but we're definitely not Brummies. We have our own flag, set of dialects and recognisable cultural artefacts, arenas and personas and yet no one can really settle on where the region begins and ends. This, coupled with its post-industrial position means that the landscape and genius loci is one of marginality and liminality.

Liminal space and identity is connected with shamanic ritual too. Anthropologists, Arnold van Gennep and Victor Turner, think about rites of passage. Turner states:

> Van Gennep has shown that all rites of transition are marked by three phases: separation; margin (or *Limen*) and aggregation. The first phase of separation comprises symbolic behaviour signifying the detachment of the individual or group either from an earlier fixed point in the social structure or a set of cultural conditions (a "state"); during the intervening liminal period, the state of the ritual subject (the" passenger") is ambiguous; he passed through a realm that has few or none of the attributes of the past or

coming state; in the third phase the passage is consummated.[24]

In Turner's reading of Van Gennep's work, young ephebes, at a certain age, lose their place as children in the tribe. They are sent out to a liminal location - often described in terms of vision quests, fasting, pilgrimages. They then become adult, shaman, warrior, poet. This passage is outside of normal codes, it is necessarily rebellious. The liminal is connected with transformation and transition, allowing for transgressive and subversive acts.

Liminality has also received attention in geography, where critics think of place, space and landscape as in-between or as transitional, and in terms of the movements and positions of people within those environments. Natasha Rogelja discusses wetlands and seashores as the 'interface between dry land and the sea and, as such, are both land and water, subject to a daily and seasonal rhythm of tidal movement'.[25] She also addresses the individual and the communal within liminal landscapes, saying 'the liminal has in recent decades been connected to the

---

[24] Victor W. Turner, 'Betwixt and Between: The Liminal Period in: "Rites de Passage"', in *The Forest of Symbols: Aspects of Ndembu Ritual*, (New York: Cornell University Press, 1967), p.94

[25] Natasha Rogelja, 'Introduction' to Hazel Andrews and Les Roberts (eds.) *Liminal Landscapes. Travel, Experience and Spaces In-between Contemporary Geographies of Leisure, Tourism and Mobility Series* (London: Routledge, 2012) P146

widespread notions of fluid or hybrid culture' going on to think about our contemporary lives as 'a permanent liminality'.[26] Some impressive thinkers in the GeoHumanities over the last decade have sought out the liminal in terms of Friction and Flow, Universal and Particular, Mobility and Stasis, and indeed layers of meaning-making (what is between?).

The connections between industry and community, and between industrial community and Geology are important and fascinating intellectual pathways – often rhizomatous in nature. Rhizomatous, like the foundations of geopoetry – it seeks out its modes of meaning making and expression through an archipelago formed disciplinarity. The liminal ground of McKay's crossing point; the natural realm of transformational elucidation. It's not just the Geological significance of the region that enables these poetics, it's the gorgeous slippery nature of Black Countryness which mirrors the gorgeous slippery slopes of geopoetry.

The things we do know for sure, or at least imagine for sure, is that Black Country identity and spaces are bound up in the forges, steelworks, glassworks, nail makers and chain makers – what was called The Cradle of the Industrial Revolution. This was enabled by the coal seams and rich mineral resources in the

---

[26] Rogelja, p.145

region. These grounds, like the chain coral, built webs of housing estates, worker's institutes, pubs and religious places – solid communal chain links. Solid and lost – another in-between – like the geology beneath the surface.

These overlooked, liminal grounds are ripe for entering and re-entering to bring about that topological reverie that Kenneth White discussed, and to look into building McKay's poetic crossing point.

The Geosites in the Black Country are exemplars for this; these are lands where one might lose their footing, both literally and imaginatively. They are beautiful, rich havens of the natural, but know where and how to look and their liminal qualities come to the fore too. Here is where prehistoric relics rest; blumenbachii, crinoid, sea lily locked in fossil time-traps. Time and space changes can be mapped in the varves, lines and layers of differently coloured rocks that pierce through the grounds and form valleys and cliffs. Stare for long enough at Wren's Nest ripple beds and one is rushed with awe in realising – physically touching and sensing - that 420 million year ago this land was a tropical ocean. Hallett realises this geological sublime too; "Stones give me here, HERE, a sense of hereness – they are like a plunge into the world itself. Hold a stone and you hold thirty, forty, fifty million years in the palm of your hand".[27] These relics humble us.

The Industrial past musters similar sensations. Ruins of engine houses, railway lines and mine shafts are everywhere in the Geopark. Eerie in their new setting; they are absent from the sensory and communal things associated with industry. Weird in their newly re-wilded home; they are off-kilter, out of place, out of time. Again, investigating the heritage in these sites gives one the sense of connectedness to our forebears and ancestors. It provides a deeper understanding and connection to the modernity and mundanity that surrounds places like Barrow Hill or Buckpool.

What we have in these spaces is a primordial limen between prehistory, industry and our everyday realms. This limen is now embedded with Wild roots. They are home to rare species of newt, dragonfly and wildflower. Places for dog walks and family picnics, bird watching and conservation. The untamed natural has returned to the rich geo-topography and taken back that which once plundered it. All this layering of different ghosts and growths are set next to domestic life. For example, Saltwells Nature Reserve is orbited by Netherton's housing estates and Merry Hill Shopping Centre. These places that hold

---

[27] Hallett, p. 69

so much symbolic and scientific treasure, that connect us to the earth and our history, do so on the doorsteps of normal everyday realms.

What we get here is a series of rhizomes of Place-identity markers. Fossil, foxglove, bell pits and terraced house all share space. Caught in a beautiful in-between. This is a post-industrial sublime.

5.

Place-identity is a term used for the ways we attach ourselves to our locales. Places are packed full of different things – smells, sounds, memories, activities, movements, people, artefacts – all site-specific – which the subject takes into their sense of self. Place is fundamental to selfhood. The bottom line of that is the land, the makeup of the rocks and soils that allow all these things to bloom. In recognising this we are awestruck at our mutual connectedness as well as our grand insignificance. Environmental Psychology considers how we connect with places and how important that is to our sense of self. Using this as a point of departure for Geopoetic exploration, I suggest that our geological heritage is the foundation stone of place-identity.

Place-Identity was coined by Harold Proshansky who defined it as:

> a sub-structure of the self-identity of the person consisting of, broadly conceived, cognitions about the physical world in which the individual lives. These cognitions represent memories, ideals, feelings, attitudes, values, preferences, meanings, and conceptions of behavior and experience which relate to the variety and complexity of physical settings […] consisting of places, spaces and their properties which have served instrumentally in the satisfaction of the

person's biological, psychological, social, and cultural needs.[28]

This web of signs, symbols, objects and moods connects us to our locales and becomes a totem for how we see ourselves in the world. We are deeply and intrinsically embedded in our physical and cultural landscapes. We are anchored. We are embodied in our geographies. Our landscapes bring about an embodied cognitive awareness of our sense of self. They support the culture and community we exist in and push out from. Place-identity then, is a profound and deep connection that anchors us, mirrors our subjecthood and marks out our identity.

What is the root of this web of place? I say, the land itself. Shepherds, farmers, blacksmiths, steelworkers, prospectors and shipbuilders all made choices about where to settle based on what usefulness might be found in the soils, and importantly, the rocks beneath, whose minerals feed and honeycomb our locales. Our nomadic hunter-gatherer ancestors did the same with their explorations of place too. From these mineral based choices bred communities and cultures, and over time bred place-identity. Geology is destiny. This has been repeated in

---

[28] Proshansky, H., Fabien, A.K., and Kaminoff, R , 1983, 'Place Identity: Physical World Socialization of the Self', Journal of Environmental Psychology, 3, p. 57–83:59

varying ways many times by a great number of great thinkers and writers. As one delves into the make-up of the land, as a Geopoet is want to do, we may find that it's the geological part of this web of signs that allows these identity-markers to yield. In fact, Geopoetics' fundamental aim is to explore and consider the connections and clashes between Being and Ground. "In this space," White asserts, "we have one foot in human society (inhabited space, inscribed), and the other in the cosmos, chaos-cosmos, chaosmos, non-human".[29] Just being in the geosites, gaining what White called the 'topological presence' is inspiring. But dig into the earth, search out your own Dudley Bug, and you're in a state of reverence, wonderment, joy and terror.

---

[29] White, K., 'The Atlantic Coast' from *The International Institute of Geopoetics: Geopeotics Notebooks*, https://www.institut-geopoetique.org/fr/cahiers-de-geopoetique/29-le-littoral-atlantique

6.

Simon Armitage, my first poetry crush, has spoken about literature's relationship with geography and earth sciences, suggesting that the story and the poem are sort of cousins to geography since 'in British Literature a sense of place and a sense of geography permeates pretty much everything'[30] and that geography and landscape 'characterise' it.

My secondary school geography teacher, Mr Reynolds, explained to our class why he loved the subject and why he thought we would too. He did this as a sort of geeky confession that kickstarted our GCSE learning. He explained that there was something beautiful and amazing to be seen in the everyday; that the study was a way of changing one's perceptions. Once you learn, even a little, about the makeup of the terrains in which we live it is impossible to just see a hill, a grass verge, a housing estate; they become carefully orchestrated, even poetic things. These things, often passed at speed and without deliberation when moving through the mundane, become Corries, Glaciofluvial Sands, Meltwater Ridges, sites centred around ancient religious or cultural symbols, social patterns that mirror their geological histories.

---

[30] Armitage, S., in *Introduction to Writing Britain: Wastelands to Waterlands*
https://www.youtube.com/watch?v=yrCCF3IMN2k&list=PL54EFE 6FD674126C1&index=4

What Mr Reynolds was explaining in his confession was Rimbaudian – *The poet becomes a seer by the prodigious and rational, disordering of the senses* – a reawakening, re-finding, refining, renaming of the familiar. These become – are brought into being by the seer as – things of movement and narrative. Eric Magrane sees 'geography, as an edge discipline (physical / social sciences as well as humanities), [that has] even more to offer a poetics engaged with the ongoing paradox of the twenty-first century'.[31] Mr Reynolds' nerdy-visonaryism struck deep and stayed with me (I'm probably not the only ex-pupil of his that has felt this which is testament to his pedagogical excellence); I went on to study Geography at A-Level, Environmental Psychology during my PhD, and have remained fascinated and awestruck by what can be achieved through acute observation of the everyday, the fusion of scientific, social and poetic mindscapes. Isn't that fusion what we're built from? Isn't that awe what we seek meaning in? Isn't its life (since these things are ecosystems) lifegiving itself?

This is a fundamental element to geopoetics – a search of the known, bringing about the unknown and using that to exfoliate (to use a geological term) one's modernity-blinkered perceptions of the world. A return to the earth – returning in

---

[31] Magrane, E, 'Introduction' from *Geopoetics in Practice* (New York: Routledge, 2020) 3

Rimabud's Drunken Boat. For this Black Country Geopoetics, it is necessary to get deeper, to go deeper, to try to find the bedrock of place. Into geology. Graham Worton, Chairman of the BCGS and Keeper of Geology for Dudley appreciates this geopoetic position too. His geological expertise, alongside his passion for his locale has imbibed him with profound understanding of the way the history of the land makes decisions for us, allows us to make social and cultural movements, and how it connects us to different parts of the globe. In his thoughts about the rainfall over the region, he notices how the lay of the land connects this overlooked place to Hull, Nottingham, Bristol.[32] He talks about the role that place-specific rock formations play in inviting populations to settle, work, build community and entrepreneurial spirit. In his narration for the Black Country Geopark Story he recognises the drama and narrative embedded in the landscape, and importantly considers what the Black Country might be like next – "That's for future generations to define, and for the planet to give us; a new era to inhabit".[33] As such, his delving into the layers of land provides a deep time and longwave

---

[32] Worton, G., *Looking Over Wren's Nest, Dudley*,
https://www.youtube.com/watch?v=m7AR0ssgmEs

[33] Worton, G., *Black Country Geopark Story*,
https://www.youtube.com/watch?v=PaxRX8-c2fU

context to our understanding of place – what Kenneth White might call a topological reverie.

I've made the geo of geopoetics Geological in my work. To get to the foundation stone of place – from where it all grew. Then, like Worton, fusing this with my Black Country passion and understanding of environmental psychological states. In this, digging deep, as deep as a poet can, physically and symbolically, and harnessing its yield to the patterns of contemporary Black Country Place-identity – as wild and as simple as they might be.

This reconfiguring of the everyday and fusion of different ways of seeing as routes towards geopoetic awe is shared by another important figure in the field – Normal Bissell – I'll let him have the last word; "It's about a poetic approach to the world, by way of sharpening our senses, being more acutely sensitive to our surroundings, developing a well-grounded, creative response to everything around us. Writing poems? Yes, but also walking hills, exchanging ideas, cutting peat, making maps – washing dishes?"[34]

---

[34] Bissell, N., *Open World Poetics*, Edinburgh Review, 88, 1992, http://www.alastairmcintosh.com/general/resources/2008-Kenneth-White-Geopoetics.pdf p.180

Faces in the rock

In the vaults
of Dudley Volcano,
mosses and lichens fuse
with flickering sunlight
and masonry. Sometimes
you see it smile. Stay
a little longer
and you hear it too –
a fuzzy clatter-clack
just below the surface;
a muted cackle of rail,
sleepers, shrinking, springing.

Petrologic Cinquain .2

Beryl,
aqua, dove, rose
of cyclosilicate –
entrenchment deep in mud tuff schist:
Maxixe.

Tourist Tracks

Wren's Nest ripple beds
gawp back at tourist gawping
in brown leaf models,
unaware of permanent
dead insignificancies.

Overhanging

Olistoliths slump-slide
as resisting stresses buckle
and atavistic avalanches – submarine,
like hangover guilt:
that dew-drenched dawn
when we grazed feet
along New Year frosts
and we didn't speak a word
and we didn't hold hands
and we didn't see anyone
and badgers were hibernating
just like the trees - seem unstill.
Up Dolerite dyke, the Heathen Coal
underhung in extract where brittle
bramble waits dusk-strike. She says,
there's something in the extraction,
something seeding, imbedding, gulfing us.

Snipers

In walks, consider
not that which catches vision,
but those hiding beings
spreading vision back at you;
pulling in fossil pulses.

Feldspar

Thick coal seams smell cool
as damp asterophyllites
petrified in Moorcroft's
clinker rock mazes. Steve
strides here. Peering at pools
housing pig minerals
slag-heaped in wind-whispered
waters, sighs, pulls path back
to Darlaston bedsit before bats
pluck dusk skimming insects.
Steve's basalt is tea stained
mattress – orthopedic, prescribed
since the crash; *'e's spines cog'avered,*
like Walsall ripple beds. He sinks
as still leaves, set in pigeonite feldspar,
float in flow sets.

7.

The Mind Seemed to Grow Giddy By Looking So Far Into The Abyss of Time[35]

This quotation is from John Playfair's observation of James Hutton's work and echoes the sublime experience of geopoetic travel and perception. The Black Country Geopark is a group of rich, lush and mysterious places; drifting through them with a geopoetic lens has profoundly impacted my own sense of place and heightened my passion for this region's history and culture. There is something special and astonishing in the experience of getting lost and being awestruck in sites that are just outside or on the edges of our everyday realms.

Take West Park in Wolverhampton – here you'll find huge glacial erratics pitched in the park grounds like ancient totems. They travelled hundreds of miles during the glacial epoch and are older still. A poignant reminder of the toddlerdom of humanity on Earth. You can touch this piece of ancient movements where kids play football, where dog walkers and joggers circulate, just minutes from Wolverhampton's bustle. The same can be said of Hayes Cutting; a fascinating dipping sequence tucked behind a rusted rail on the Industrial Estates

---

[35] *Playfair, John (1805).* "Hutton's Unconformity". *Transactions of the Royal Society of Edinburgh. V (III).*

48

of The Lye. Commuters, deliveries, school runs zip passed as it sits in almost invisibility.

There is something atavistic in these sites, or something that summons and imbues atavism. I don't mean this in any negative way; I see it as a touchstone for reconnecting with our locales, lands and the Earth in a deep time context and with the tactile knowledge that runs down to the oldest parts of our biology. Alyson Hallett recognises this in her evaluations of human cultures' relationship to stones; "Since we've been on this planet, as humans, we've paid attention to the patterns of stars and the spirits that live in stones".[36] This, I think, is what White was talking about when he said "The geopoeticist is immediately placed in the enormous" or when Francis Ponge stated "they sink into the night of logos" or when George Amar thinks about the embodied knowledge of reading the land: "reading is like swimming or dancing [...] eskimos can read snow and nomads desert sand".[37] These are things that we can walk through, touch, see and smell, and in that, connect us to our region and our land in ways that are both intellectual and

---

[36] Hallett, p. 13

[37] Amar, G., 'From Surrealism to Geopoetics' from *The International Institute of Geopoetics: Geopoetic Notebooks*, https://www.institut-geopoetique.org/fr/cahiers-de-geopoetique/118-du-surrealisme-a-la-geopoetique

visceral. It is, like ancient wayfinding skills, embodied and physical wisdom.

Robert Brechon discusses the relationship between cognition and feeling and between self and landscape in context to Fernando Pessoa's *Book of Tranquillity*:

> [F]rom the end of the first paragraph, something shatters in the vision of the landscape. The exaltation of color, light and night turns against itself and falls back into the abyss of self-awareness. Intelligence takes over from emotion, which it unmasked after having caught it in the act of posing and imposture. All the symbols that the landscape suggests to the mind of the walker, far from filling it, complete the disenchantment. He can neither absorb the landscape nor let himself be absorbed by it. His conscience overflows the landscape on all sides, as the landscape overflows from his consciousness. There is no possible identification or consubstantiality between the mind and the world.[38]

This dissolution of subjecthood and agency turns into an act of revitalising with the grounds. Thought collides with the sensory data, being collides with earth, and something bigger than the sum of its parts springs forth in the conjugation. We

---

[38] Brechon, R., 'Landscapes by Fernando Pessoa' from *The International Institute of Geopoetics: Geopoetic Notebooks*, https://www.institut-geopoetique.org/fr/cahiers-de-geopoetique/28-paysages-de-fernando-pessoa

drift into ideas of pilgrimage and shamanism here. The medicine man or witch doctor who travels – physically, psychically and spiritually - transforming themselves and their landscapes as they do and bringing back wisdom and cures to the community.

Pilgrimage is a walk out of the daily and known, into the landscape and into oneself - the hard worked trekking acts as personal and spiritual sacrifice that pays for the widened wisdom of self and place. In both cases we walk into the sacred. Sally Welch describes it as something 'not simply concerned with the journeys of those physically travelling but as a way of living and thinking'.[39] The movement through landscape enables experience and thought, being and space, to harmonise. In Christian practices pilgrimage began when 'the first disciples rushed to see for themselves the place where Jesus had been buried and was no longer present'[40] and runs through the Old Testament in stories of migration, exodus and evacuation. In each story we see the physicality of movement and land meeting the transcendental or supernatural of soul and heaven. In each story we see the hard-won battle of arduous journeying resulting in illumination and emancipation. We see landscapes

---

[39] Welch, S., *Pilgrimage: Pilgrimage for Walkers and Armchair Travellers* (Abingdon: The Bible Readers Fellowship, 2017)
[40] Welch

and mindscapes shifting and reaching new peaks of awareness. Welch's text offers a similar route whereby several Pilgrimage Routes are mapped out as personal reflection, historic journalism and religious meditation. The geopoet, kin to the pilgrim, touches the sacred within the terrestrial – the grounding and the lands themselves bring about wisdom / poetics. Placing these journeys in a mytho-geological context, much like the work of David Montgomery.[41]

Iain Sinclair talks about his deep topography in these terms too – deliberately seeking out overlooked spaces, working towards an idiosyncratic vision or sense of place, and sees these acts as a form of poetics. In a lecture at De Montfort University Sinclair spoke about his walk around the M25 and its relationship to developing a creative process. He calls it a "Fugue" and a "Psychic Commando Course", suggesting that when walking or drifting:

> There's a sense of possession, there's a sense of pilgrimage, there's a sense of allowing place to pour through you and channel itself through you until you achieve a voice. You walk out of yourself in the way John Clare, the poet, talked of walking out of his knowledge. His knowledge was of this very specific locale [...] In a sense the walk is a poem: the energy that promotes you into that is a way of dealing with

---

[41] See Montgomery's *The Rocks Don't Lie: A Geologist Investigates Noah's Flood* (London: W N Norton, 2012)

these psychological pressures, pressures of history and territory that all become resolved through the physical act of finding the right form of writing.[42]

Hallett talks about her poetics in light of this possession of place or land too. Considering it as a route towards unlocking ancient, embodied wisdoms:

> I suspect that when I work I am listening to my animal self, my uncivilised self, the lizard that still inhabits the core of my brain [...] I am listening to the voices of the dead [...] the voices in the wind. The voices in stones. If I think about it too much, it's disturbing. If I don't think too much, it's just my life.[43]

This observation is shared by Pierre Jamet who says "It is an experience of place leading to a no-where and bringing back to places: *topos, a-topia, pan-topia*".[44] Tucker, drawing on Tungusic languages, recognises the roots of the word Shaman connected to Saman. In this etymological journey, the Shaman is "one who is excited, moved, raised" or in a state where one

---

[42] Iain Sinclair, *Waywardness, Writing and Place*, from https://www.youtube.com/watch?v=JIYBYlZhyg4, published 06/06/2014

[43] Hallett, p. 15

[44] Jamet, P., 'Kenneth Whte and Religion' from *Grounding a World: Essays on the Work of Kenneth White*, eds Bowd, G., Forsdick, C., Bissell, N., (Alba Editions: 2005) p. 104

"know[s] in an ecstatic manner".[45] Tucker discusses how White speaks of journeys and being in the world as "walking one's way into a deeper, fresher sense of the pulse of life".[46] The geopoet, like the Shaman, is entering the *other* dimension and this, like the trance inducing prayers and chants of these ancient religious practices, is done so "through a spatial poetics which has emptiness at its centre – but the sort of emptiness which is at the same time a plentitude" in an attempt to "reconnect one with a much more cosmically-oriented sense of *world*, of life's deepest energies and potentialities".[47]

Geopoetic shamanism and pilgrimage sees the land as part of one's ancestry; acts that bring about primal ancestral wisdom / consciousness in us. Hallet argues that "everywhere we go we are walking on everything and everyone who has gone before. We build our buildings on the bodies, the bones, the blood of our relatives".[48] Robert MacFarlane's[49] work illuminates the importance of stories held in the land too – like memories and

[45] Tucker, 'Space, Energy, Light: The Shamanic Element in the Work of Kenneth White' from *Grounding a World: Essays on the Work of Kenneth White*, eds Bowd, G., Forsdick, C., Bissell, N., (Alba Editions: 2005) p.82

[46] Tucker, p.81

[47] ibid

[48] Hallett, p.80

[49] See *Underland, Spell Songs, Landmarks, The Old Ways, The Wild Places*

folklore passed through paths. We are walking on all of these things on the momentary surfaces of earth's deep time underbelly.

Patterns of this geopoetic journeying and its connection with Shamanism are cross-cultural and transcend epoch and continent. Timothy Freke's collection of interviews with Shamans across the world offer fascinating connections and similarities. In his introduction he argues:

> Shamanism reminds us of the fragile beauty of the web of life; that creation is not a resource to be coerced into fulfilling our insatiable appetites, but a living wonder to be respected. It roots us in our common mother the Earth; reawakening an awareness of all living things as her extended family [...] Shamanism refreshes ancient memories of harmonious human community and offers us hope [...] It teaches us to reach below the surface of modern superficialities and reconnect with something old and mysterious within the depths of our soul.[50]

Malidoma Patrice Some from the West African Dagara Tradition, suggests that "Shamanism is a response to the challenge of understanding the language of the invisible world

---

[50] Freke, T., 'Inrodution' *Shamanic Wisdomkeepers: Shamanism in the Modern World* (New Alresford: Godsfield Press, 1999)

as it transpires into the visible world".[51] A re-grounding and re-finding of the worldly / earthy experience and expression through delving into the unknown – which persists in the known. This is akin to attempting to remove the modernity forged blinkers that separate us from our sense of world. Some also argues that "spirits are different layers of intelligence and powers".[52] Again, there is the sense of burrowing into the layers of time-space, of knowledge and of being – a spiritual geology that might bring us "closer to a cosmic state of reality".[53]

Miguel A. Kavlin's Amazonian shamanism relies on similar geopoetic-esque principles. He says, "Everywhere in the world has the sun and the moon in the sky, the earth beneath us, the four directions all around us. So these are the main forces that shamans all over the world work with".[54] His practice uses the psychedelic Ayahuasca plant to help "reconnect with mythical time and space".[55] This sentiment is similar to notions of delving into Deep Time, in seeking a "topological presence" and

[51] Some, M. P., Interviewed in *Shamanic Wisdomkeepers: Shamanism in the Modern World* (New Alresford: Godsfield Press, 1999) ed Timothy Freke, p.27

[52] Some, p.33

[53] ibid

[54] Kavlin, M. A., Interviewed in *Shamanic Wisdomkeepers: Shamanism in the Modern World* (New Alresford: Godsfield Press, 1999) p.41

[55] Kavlin, p.45

in "sinking into the night of logos". This mythical time, ephemeral and New Age as it may sound, could very well be the sense of touching base with the eons of Earth's phases, the awe-stricken recognition of the toddlerdom of humanity and our wide-stemming interconnections. Kavlin calls us to "re-establish whatever connections we can; to know that we can feel the earth always underneath our feet".[56]

Lama Khemsar Rinpoche in the Tibetan Yungrung Bon Tradition believes in Nagas; mischievous but guiding spirits. According to Rinpoche the word Naga means serpent and in Tibet they're called sadak-lu-nyen. "'Sadak' literally means landowner. Nagas are the owners of the land, nature, the trees, the water, the earth and so forth".[57] In communing with these entities, Tibetan Shamans are connecting with spirits of place within the nonhuman realms. They learn their place in the world and elsewhere. This communication comes from reverence with the anima of the natural forces. This is White's *enormous* and *exformation*. This is Amar's *Erotic of the Earth*.

Andy Baggott works within the Celtic Tradition and says:

---

[56] Kavlin, p.51

[57] Rinpoche, L. K., Interviewed in *Shamanic Wisdomkeepers: Shamanism in the Modern World* (New Alresford: Godsfield Press, 1999) p.71

For me Shamanism is an attitude toward life more than a philosophy or a religion. It's running your life with respect and interaction – very much an Earth-based way of working [...] I go and commune with nature. That changes my consciousness and my thought patterns, and solutions that I hadn't seen with my western consciousness suddenly become apparent.[58]

Altering consciousness through contact with the earth echoes White's diagnosis of how we "let be" outside, bringing about ontological change. One of the main drives of geopoetics is to *leave the motorway of modern life*. It is the blinkers and the poisons of our current ways of being that stop us connecting and grounding in the necessary ways. Grounding and re-finding become combats against anthropocentrism and disconnection. We remove obstacles between self and nature, intellect and intuition, we remove life's toxins – Blake's Mind Forged Manacles. Baggott says: "toxins have an effect of ungrounding you [...] the more grounded you are the higher the realms you can get to".[59] At the heart of these Shamanics is the terrestrial – being and land, landscape / mindscape.

---

[58] Baggot, A., Interviewed in *Shamanic Wisdomkeepers: Shamanism in the Modern World* (New Alresford: Godsfield Press, 1999) pp. 83-85
[59] Baggot, p.87

Martin Prechtel from the Tzutujil Mayan Trad is an Acjun, which means a person who goes looking. He calls rocks by their sacred names and knows how to talk to them. He says, "Shamans are technicians [...] technicians of the holy", and sees his job as "reconnecting westerners to their deep indigenous souls".[60] We can read this as a geopoetic realigning of the self in the earth. We "go" as in move, and we "look" as in re-sense.

The evidence of the effects of being in green spaces in improving wellbeing and mental health is now overwhelming. In terms of evolutionary biology, "our late arrival into cities might help explain our affinity with nature and green spaces".[61] Edward O. Wilson coined the term, "Biophilia".[62] His hypothesis is that our primal landscapes shaped our brains to be alert to the particularity of different environments – attached to our basic survival drives of seeking food, water and safety. These neurological and biological networks reward us, sending dopamine cues that enhanced survival for our ancestors. When

[60] Prechtel, M., Interviewed in *Shamanic Wisdomkeepers: Shamanism in the Modern World* (New Alresford: Godsfield Press, 1999) pp.106-107

[61] Douglas, K. and Douglas, J., 'Green Spaces aren't just for Nature' from *The New Scientist*, 24/03/2021, https://www.newscientist.com/article/mg24933270-800-green-spaces-arent-just-for-nature-they-boost-our-mental-health-too/

[62] Wilson, E., *Biophilia* (Cambridge, MA: Harvard University Press, 1982)

we're close to a beautiful river for example, we may feel emotional responses connected to its beauty, power, and peacefulness – and these are brought about through a multitude of sensory data. Our neurological pathways and nervous system are triggering ancient responses too: it's telling us *well done, you found food and cleanliness and water and now you and yours can survive.* Wilson argued that this is why being in nature makes us feel good. Wilson said 'our spirit is woven from it, hopes rise on its currents'.[63] This is because 'For millions of years humans simply went at nature with everything they had [...] it enhanced the genetic evolution of the brain and generated more and better culture'.[64] Still now, in our hyper modern states there are landscape/mindscapes we can inhabit to bring this about; 'It is a frontier literally at our fingertips, and the one for which our spirit appears to have been explicitly designed'.[65] This terrestrial shamanism has biological, cellular and molecular scaffolding.

The New Scientist reports that "the past few years have seen an explosion of research finding concrete links between increased exposure to nature and not just improved physical

---

[63] Wilson, 1

[64] Wilson, 13

[65] Wilson, 21

health, but better mental health, too".[66] In a 2019 PNAS published study,[67] academics from Denmark's University of Aarhus found that childhood exposure to green space – parks, forests, rural lands, etc. – reduces the risk for developing an array of psychiatric disorders during adolescence and adulthood. This is the largest epidemiological study to date, establishing the important connection. Almost as amazing as the headline discovery is the fact that those who spend more time in green space have greater mental health benefits. A simple internet search produces an enormous list of peer-reviewed cross-referenceable research produced by the world's most impressive scientists. Dobson et al, "call for attention to the 'magic of the mundane' under-valued but essential everyday experiences, in supporting human wellbeing".[68] Keniger et al discuss thirty years of health research in their 2013 paper,[69] and Hough RL considers this research in context

[66] Douglas, K. and Douglas, J., 'Green Spaces aren't just for Nature'

[67] Engemann K,et al 'Residential green space in childhood is associated with lower risk of psychiatric disorders from adolescence into adulthood'. Proc Natl Acad Sci U S A. 2019 Mar 12; 116(11):5188-5193. doi: 10.1073/pnas.1807504116. Epub 2019 Feb 25. PMID: 30804178; PMCID: PMC6421415.

[68] Dobson et al, 'The Magic of the Mundane: The Vulnerable Web of Connections Between Urban Nature and Wellbeing' from *Cities*, Vol:108, Jan 2021, 102989

[69] What are the benefits of interacting with nature? *International Journal of Environmental Research and Public Health*, 2013, vol. 10 (pg. 913-935)

to the variety of exposure and types of environment.[70] The physical benefits are tracked and linked to mental health benefits too, in studies such as Hartig T, Mang M, Evans GW.[71] and Ratcliffe E, Gatersleben B, Sowden PT. study of bird song.[72]

Being in green spaces provides a rush of fresh air, raised heart rate and kickstarts the sympathetic nervous system. This, alongside the differences we perceive from *usual* environments and *normal* navigation processes, produces a refocusing of mind and heightened alertness. What we're triggering in this combination of perceptive-sensory and cardiovascular shifting is connected to our fight or flight mechanisms; of acute focus and awareness and preparedness to move. Yet again, this connects with survival processes deep in our bodies' histories and we are rewarded. All of this has profound effects on one's neurology and reconfigures the biology – we, and the earth, remind our bodies of the primal functions. Or as Pretchell says, "It's getting people back to their roots".[73] Moving this back to

---

[70] Hough, R. L., Biodiversity and human health: Evidence for causality?, *Biodiversity and Conservation*, 2014, vol. 23 (pg. 267-288)

[71] Hartig et al, 'Restorative effects of natural environment experiences' from *Environment and Behavior*, 1991, vol. 23 (pg. 3-26)

[72] Ratcliffe et al, 'Bird sounds and their contributions to perceived attention restoration and stress recovery' from *Journal of Environmental Psychology*, 2013, vol. 36 (pg. 221-228)

[73] Prechtel, P.107

poetry and geography, poet, Craig Santos Perez remarks, 'conceptions of geography teach us that the earth is the sacred source of all life, and all beings are interconnected in a complex kinship network'.[74]

It seems Totem is exactly the right word for West Park's erratics, and I'd use it for the geological cuttings and other features across the region too: that which, with a strange sense of animism, calls and connects people and place.

[74] Santos Perez, C, 'Introduction' from *Geopoetics in Practice* (New York: Routledge, 2020) 5

Bibble #2

She said, *iss just a rock,*
and she was right. *Yo'm*
right, me wench,
an' thass the rub,
iss just a rock, beginning
wi' clast grains swept
into colloids, rushed
wi' winds an' rains
an' ice racings, then holts,
compresses. He sees his eye
in hers as iris reflects dune glass
with tropopause and halite.

Petrologic Cinquain .3

Red mud,
laterite soils
plundered by strip mining
and Bayered for pale gallium:
Bauxite.

Little Girl Lost

She scrambles sunken
hoarstones – grass verged
snaefellsnes dotting
Northycote Farm. Her
toddler toes tracking labile
Pleistocene. Norfolk Blacks
and Guineafowl flock dew
drenched field - staccato
plucking scattered above
knocker grounds where she scales
shrouded lithologies. Dad repeats
careful, slowly, easy, careful
then hears himself in protean
conjunctions and stops, smiles,
watches a second of time martyr
in tantric tremor. The earth rises
from sleep, from caverns deep
where life conveyed.

Little Girl Found

To this day they dwell
In a lonely dell,
Nor fear the wolvish howl
Nor the lion's growl.
WILLIAM BLAKE

Tabulae colonies helix
in plankton hunts. Almost
still. Almost silent. Mirrors
fresh covens of fungi, sharing
overlooked ground now dried
across eranthams. Our girl,
in her own pullulation, collects
stoned arthropods from dried
beds. We spent toddlerdom
place-stamping wayfind skills.
Er loffs when er's turned around, er does,
our wench loves the spiral unraveling
in mapping stray routes home. Blake's
little girl found finds herself in father's
footsteps, helixed in every inch and pore -
even absent from each they slink in tune
to chain coral's infinite coda.

Thursday: Beacon Hill Quarry

Our Roy said *iss scarred –*
beautymarked by beacon fires,
Wrottersley's luna scopings.
He shepherds limestone ways,
lighting lens on knapweed, carline
ox-tongue, heeding optic glares
against hairstreak flutterings.
Roy said, *they'm rare, our kid,*
rare beauts on beautmarked mount.
Thass why Sedgley Morrismen come
circlin' among whitsun flames.
Yo' cor ave a beacon wi'out watchmen.
He lays the ley's spine, supporting
steep steps. Sunrays make dirt glimmer,
magnifies silty mudstone and brown lime,
lagoon shallowed in Gorstian days (if earth bones
know what days mean) and further to skeletal
stems of sea lily, bryophyte, velvet worm. Concestors,
hand holding, forward facing, tracing and traced in
Thunor's forge, like me and my shepherd.

On Wolverhampton Road, we stop for fags at the BP
and sup a pint at the Mount Pleasant. He grandads me.
Reaches into pocket, hands me three black
bubbled bibbles of clinker. *Tarra'abbit* he says.

Fens

Between white washed estate
where terraced streets named
Milton, Byron, Tennyson
and the green-sludged end
of the cut, sits half-dried
menace: Fens Pool. Shoveler,
Signet, Gadwall blether about
with the gypsy youths toying
oss and trap, brothers scrambling
quarry ridges, the statuesque drip
of lonesome fishermen. A cut through.
A twitcher's hide. A limen for fights
and fucks, shits and shifts. Megaliths
penetrate loam's maidenhead –
fireclay peeks from seatearth
at ruined colliery pillars
and reservoir banks, and father/daughter
are sniper-still as broad bodied chaser
peels from pupae in adder tongues.

Exfoliation

Ridged, she raised
wedding ring down
Rowley microgabbro:
rock, like rhino pelt,
brittle as bird egg.

Days counted with maps,
hours in ups and downs,
minutes are meters,
seconds - surveys. Each
calculated in back-forths.

Stillness still sleeps in this pattern;
take the rock sealed ammonite
unearthed that long afternoon
when sun scorched shoulders
hunched over on Blue Rock –
our tiny blumenbachii. We plot
it in our collection - date, time, site
stamped. Memory stores/stirs it.

It's the soft float of wan stars
and stripes, rooted to the moon;
never still in its chartered zone.

Turned, she slips
Samson slope back to
Oakham estates. Rocks
in pockets crumble, reveal
miniature contours. Pale rims
around untouched fingers.

8.

PALIMPSEST:

Something reused or altered but still bearing visible traces of its earlier form.

Something having usually diverse layers or aspects apparent beneath the surface

Above are two dictionary definitions for the term Palimpsest; a term often discussed in association with Robert MacFarlane's book, *Underland*, to consider the makeup of our landscapes and, importantly, the nature of our cognition as we journey into it. This is a deep time exploration of layers and traces. Layers that underpin our everyday. Traces of everyday prior to ours. MacFarlane's work has been instrumental to my poetics during this project. I've been an admirer of his musical writing that burrows into the cracks between the wild and the human and the mythical for a long time. This is a literary preoccupation stemming from the Romantics of the eighteenth century and that can be followed through to the uncommercial travellers of the nineteenth century and the fin de siecle flaneurs, then into the psycho-geographers that peak and trough throughout the twenty and twenty first. It is in the same spirit of this Palimpsestic Journeying that I've undertaken my Black Country Geopoetics. I see this as a psycho-geographical exercise, going out and aimlessly drifting, searching out the overlooked edgelands or interzones – the off-kilter meetings of green and grey, industrial and natural. This is in-keeping with some of the traditions of this experimental method for place-writers.

Guy Debord defined psychogeography as, "The study of the precise laws and specific effects of the geographical environment, consciously organised or not, on the emotional behaviour of individuals".[75] It focuses on urban wandering, "the imaginative reworking of the city, the otherworldly sense of spirit of place, the unexpected insights and juxtapositions created by aimless drifting, the new ways of experiencing familiar surroundings".[76] This imaginative re-working is preoccupied with the in-between: one is aimless, without usual or normal purpose; between the familiar-knowable and the novel-imagined. It's a liminal position, on the threshold of real and imagined. According to Michel de Certeau, 'this is a sort of knowledge that remains silent. Only hints of what is known but unrevealed are passed on "just between you and me.'".[77] De Certeau calls it a childlike experience, one that creates a

---

[75] Merlin Coverley, *Psychogeography: Pocket Essentials* (Harpended: Pocket Essentials, 2010), p. 90

[76] Coverley, p. 10

[77] Michel de Certeau, 'The Practice of Everyday Life', Trans. by Steven Rendall (London: University of California Press, 1988) p.108

fictional or imagined space, within the functional and real world:

> The childhood experience that determines spatial practices later develops its effects, proliferates, floods private and public spaces, undoes their readable surfaces, and creates within the planned city a "metaphorical" or mobile city, like the one Kandinsky dreamed of: "a great city built according to all the rules of architecture and then suddenly shaken by a force that defies all calculation.[78]

In his book *Pocket Essentials to Psychogeography*, Merlin Coverley paraphrases postmodernists like Jean Baudrillard and Marc Auge, when he contests that:

> the essential emptiness of modern life is obscured behind an elaborate and spectacular array of commodities and our immersion in this world of rampant consumerism leaves us disconnected from the history and community that might give our lives meaning [...] Amidst the barrage of media imagery to which we are subjected, our emotional response is blunted and we become unable to engage directly with our surroundings without the mediated images of television and advertising.[79]

So, we are what we are told and identity is formed, at least in part, from our sense of place, however, our sense of place is

---

[78] de Certeau, p.110

[79] Coverley, pp. 102-116

mediated by the agendas of postmodern life. Bleak. Furthermore, we lose the direct apprehension of life lived in locales by overstimulation and overreliance on digital realms. What now? Coverley argues, "The city must be rebuilt upon new principles that replace our mundane and sterile experiences",[80] and the way this can be done is through wandering, becoming one who "remakes the city in accordance with his own imagination [...] that seeks to overthrow the established order of the day".[81]

Michel de Certeau discusses this too, arguing that drifting 'transforms the bewitching world by which one was "possessed" into a text that lies before one's eyes. It allows one to read it, to be a solar Eye, looking down like a god'. The image of the seer or the godlike figure is important; signifying undoing the spell of the urban environment. The place as text motif harkens back to Amar's "reading" too. De Certeau continues: 'the voyeur-god created by this fiction [...] must disentangle himself from the murky intertwining daily behaviors and make himself alien to them'[82]. The pedestrian is Promethean, making stories of place, or based in places, through acts of rebellious movements. Through this 'rhetoric of walking' the psychogeographer

---

[80] Coverley, p. 84

[81] Coverley, pp. 41-42

[82] Michel de Certeau , pp. 92-93

74

uncovers the unseen and overlooked and creates new models or structures for perceiving spaces.

Drifting takes an instinctual and subjective approach to looking into one's sense of place, space and history, drawing one's own conclusions on how these affect community and how it might be challenged. The Environmental Psychologists understand the importance of preserving that which makes a place unique as a benefit for communal and individual wellbeing and wellness. Psychogeographers see drifting as a radical, political act aimed at undermining established notions of place. As such, the instinctual drifter, aware of how important place-identity is, becomes one who pushes back at the homogenisation of space and place. The geopoetic drifter, aware of the importance of grounding and the earth, 'leaves the motorway of western civilisation'. The poet, Ian Duhig, has written about this challenging of space structures within literature and mythmaking, suggesting that many narratives and conservative uses of space lay stress on:

> sticking to straight and narrow roads, avoiding distraction into backwaters and back alleys. roads are languages, as they say, and poetry has many guides now, some of whom oversimplify the terrain in the service of connecting up the landmark, a natural human tendency: Stevens wrote of how we live in descriptions of places rather than places themselves,

while Lawrence observed, "the map appears more real to us than the land".

Going on to argue in favour of Debordian drift:

> I want to put a word in for pointless travelling without landmarks [...] it can be a messy process but poetry is messy and there are invaluable things to be found in the dark that you could not discover in any other way [...] you have wonder and surprise to gain and nothing to lose but your certainties.[83]

Psychogeography challenges prescribed ideas of place, offering new notions of what it can be used for. Psychogeographers, like geopoets, offer instinctual approaches to assessing who we are and where we're from.

I'm moving away from the urban centricity of psychogeography, and rather than being totally aimless – it is a drift with a geopoetic purpose and lens. It needs to be loose and instinctual and likewise needs to have a grounding or lens to the wo/andering. Through this, I harness the idiosyncratic perspective of psychogeography, but focus it with geological observations. Marco Fazzini recognises the *derive* inhabiting geopoetic travel too, arguing that

---

[83] Duhig, I., 'Reading with Your Feet', from *Poetry Review*, Volume 102:3 Autumn (2012) (London: The Poetry Society) 106 - 109, (pp.106-109)

instead of returning to or reconquering the place where he or she moved from, multiplies his or her paths and trajectories which come to be other than 'straight'. Losing, deliberately, his or her right/straight way, and indicating no obvious direction at all in his or her peregrinations.[84]

My starting point for the Chain Coral Chorus has obvious links to the first definition of Palimpsest above. The geosites within the Black Country Geopark are rewilded places; reused and altered by time, conservation and leisure. And they hold the visible traces of earlier times and uses – mining, railways, Silurian marshes. This makes them symbolically charged with drama, symbol and narrative that stretches out for eons. Traces and layers that can be measured in a socio-historical way and through stratigraphic measurement. Webs of signs that can be linked through verifiable record, feeling and folklore – no one thing being less true or significant than the other, but working collaboratively through the topography. Using definition one as a point of departure, we enter definition two, and back on ourselves again. Such is the nature of deep time navigation.

The covid-19 situation offered a strange influence on this palimpsest travelling too. The social distancing and lockdown

---

[84] Fazzini, M., 'Kenneth Whte's Erratic Itinerary' from *Grounding a World: Essays on the Work of Kenneth White*, eds Bowd, G., Forsdick, C., Bissell, N., (Alba Editions: 2005) p.44

restrictions have forced many of us, including myself, to rethink movement. Where we go, how far we go, how often we move and who we move with have been brought to the front of our consciousness. Limitations on time, distance and variability coincide with "temporary" remodelling of place – closures, abandoned places, alienation, solitude. For many, this has narrowed our scope for travel and movement and brought a wider attention into something seemingly narrow. This "New Normal" has opened up possibilities in re-finding and reconfiguring our relationship with place and movement; forged through repetition, solitude, scope, and finding new reasons or motivations for movement. We've recalibrated, in the same way we did with scale, our direction of movement. We've been moving down, into the traces and into the layers.

Vertical Travel and MicroTravel are two subsets of this palimpsest approach. Under usual and regular circumstances, we travel horizontally; moving with functional purpose from point A to point B – onwards and returning. If we travel vertically, as coined by Kris Lackey, we burrow into the particulars of place; it's history, folklore, plant and insect life, overlooked aspects. In Microtravel, following Michael Cronin's ideas, the tiny and often repeated journey enables deep, downward observations.[85] In these non-normative movements we cast off the functional purpose and enter new states of perception – we see what has always been there in microscopic details and in doing so we understand our grounds with more specificity and on our own terms. Charles Forsdick has called vertical travel a "type of descent into the detail of place" which illuminates the "'divine detail' of the proximate and the everyday".[86] This has pertinent connections with geological observation – travelling vertically takes us into the layers of muck, soil and rock, into the earth's primal shifts and movements. We no longer see things as flat (A-B). Our temporal and sensory perceptions change.[87]

George Amar links this to a geopoetic trajectory saying:

> The Erotic of the Earth finds perhaps its most iconic form in travel. Oh there are many forms – and speeds – of travel, and the dwelling or residence, a slow form par excellence, is not the least intense. To travel is not to visit but to inhabit the earth. To live, not only

---

[85] Forsdick, C, 'Vertical Travel', from *The Routledge Research Companion to Travel Writing*, eds Alasdar Pettinger and Tim Youngs (Abingdon: Routledge, 2019)

[86] Forsdick, C., *Travel Writing in an Age of Confinement*, https://bcla.org/reflections/travel-writing-in-an-age-of-confinement/

[87] Key figures in this field are Charles Forsdick, Katherine Walchester and Zoe Kinsley. *Keywords for Travel Writing* from Anthem Press is an invaluable resource for those interested in "alternative movement".

"somewhere", but to inhabit the earth itself, to become Earth. To be a mountain, to be a river, to learn from its mists, its lightning, to feel a path, a wave, sand and grass, a bird of the air, a man of the woods, a sea bass, a mountain brigand, and even a city nomad. Man-of-the-Earth.[88]

This type of travel is one of seeking out the overlooked treasures on our doorsteps or on the edges of our everyday. A re-wayfinding that Amar covers in great detail. He says "geopoetics is the desire for a re-exploration, a re-enjoyment, a re-evaluation of the world, of the wide world. Step by step, journey by journey, sensation by sensation, flash of thought by flash of thought – remaking (groping) the map of the world".[89] This is a geopoetic equivalent to Vertical or Micro Travel; the repeated "re-" in this quotation illuminates the significance of searching the known to pull out the unknown, moving down through the layers of the landscape and traces of place to do so. Amar claims that:

> Geopoetics is inseparable from the re-discovery of this specific effect, an energy from which it draws and which it sets out to express [...] The geopoetic effect, which should not be confused with the beauty attached to such and such an object, such a being or

[88] Amar, G., 'The Meaning of the Earth' from *The International Institute of Geopoetics: Geopoetic Notebooks, https://www.institut-geopoetique.org/fr/cahiers-de-geopoetique/24-le-sens-de-la-terre*

[89] Amar, *From Surrealism to Geopoetics*

such a site, is the sign, the psycho-physiological index of a certain quality of our relation to beings-of-it.[90]

Amar touches on White's ideas of bringing together the cognitive, intellectual thought with that of the body, the senses and the instincts as a way of grounding oneself. He argues that "geopoetics is perhaps characterized by reading the world". Here, we move into the skills humanity has lost in its stepping away from the natural:

> We no longer know how to read the world because we no longer know how to read, because we believe that to read is to decipher a message [...] Of the good fisherman they say he "reads the river".[91]

It's this re-learning that brings about the sublime moment, the transcendence or the topological presence:

> In the reading of a real thing, the recognition of what that thing is, and the emotion linked to the fact that it tells us something, of itself, of the world, of ourselves, are inextricably linked [...] The Earth, "the Earth", is precisely the class of common reality of terrestrial beings. Being terrestrial: this is what we have in common, this is what we are (reciprocally) real [...] It is not a question of describing nor even (even less) of "being inspired" by the Earth, but of understanding and experiencing that it is our

---

[90] Amar, *From Surrealism to Geopoetics*

[91] Amar, *From Surrealism to Geopoetics*

"earthliness", the feeling-of-world within us, our desiring and sensitive knowledge of the Earth which is the source of the most fertile poetics [...] The geopoetic form of expression is that which restores as completely as possible to language its nature of being terrestrial.[92]

Fazzini ties this terrestrial transcendence to our current ecological debates and anthropocentric position:

This is the effect contemporary men and women are in dire need of because of the devalued relationship between 'human' and 'non-human' in our society. This is the language which can recall for us ancestral reminiscences and insights, serving as both a walking and linguistic yoga [...] where the internal landscape coincides with and faces an external one for an eternal re-symbolization of *being* in the world, thus exchanging flux and energy, steps and passages, limits and margins.[93]

We're with the Shamans again here. The erotic of the earth, found through geopoetic movement, brings about the bodily changes in breath, heart rate, perception and focus, carrying forth the ancestral wisdoms held deep in our evolutionary biologies. Furthermore, as we peer into Deep Time and geological heritage, we're reawakening on the ancestral grounds of the earth too. In touching the ancestral genius loci,

---

[92] Amar, *From Surrealism to Geopoetics*
[93] Fazzini, p.47

we re-find our being-landscape-ness. How do we reach this sense of awe stricken terrestrialness? How do we learn to read in this way? Like the Palimpsest Literary line from John Clare to Ian Sinclair – we walk. Amar suggests, "In many ways, the typical geopoetic experience is travel [...] travel is for geopoetics, far from any tourism, a sort of dream-of-reality".[94] Ann Scott links these ideas back to ancient wayfinding systems and early attempts to map our worlds and our understandings:

> The earliest concept of finding oneself came from the sky. From the star patterns of the heavens, the first traveller on the sea established a first truth, with an X on his terrestrial chart. By this lode-manage he had his bearings [...] the place he marked was 'ex-act'. That is, its source was 'ex-agon' – beyond the 'agon', the action, which is Earth. His world received its leading grace from the stars and a trusted contact was made between the agon and the ex-act place beyond it. Anything that is shaped by the wind of the sea takes on a grace, like sails or sand-dunes, or a man in need of a Way. When he sets down his place on his chart, he called it 'a reading'.[95]

[94] Amar, *From Surrealism to Geopoetics*

[95] Scott, A., 'On Exactness: Reading Kenneth White in the Twetyfirst Century, from *Grounding a World: Essays on the Work of Kenneth White*, eds Bowd, G., Forsdick, C., Bissell, N., (Alba Editions: 2005) p.168

Covering every inch of a place. Walking and rewalking in every conceivable direction and route. Every path. Every desire line. Every dead end. I've seen the Wren's Nest ripple beds and the bell pits up close, from above and from within. I've watched the same pebble accidently moved, inch by inch, by different feet over periods of weeks until it disappears into a hawthorn that casts a different shadow depending on the time of year. I've seen the slow build and fall of spring and autumn in minute detail along the same patch of woodland. Through this I've gained a flow like state, a hyper-alertness of my grounds. Through habit, through movement, through deliberate, slow, acute observations, through touching and smelling and breathing it all in, I've gained an embodied knowledge of my grounds. I bear witness and it seems to stare back. We're like a cobweb spread out in MacFarlane's underlands, signalling semaphores each to each through silken strands.

Rupture/Rapture

Rowley raggers slogged
oxidised slag from boshboil
stew, turned the earth
inside out, plucking mafic
hailstones in a bum-hul-bum-hul-
bum-hul beat. Bumblehole sub
sides with wild warren release.
Hingley's lost to Rush rushings
and Reedmace – this is the new
proving house since Coots cooped
Cobb's ruin. Searching hellish dikes
and sills here where rocks glowed
to surface, you cast shiny euhedral
finds into reddened waters, pray
the mirroring stays under.

Efts

Tek track
ovaled through 'awthorn
by fate foraging for Gornal Fish
in Gornal Grit -
Thass ow yo'll lose
yower jawbone, me wench,
wi' gawpin' gob.
Silica sands sit cool
beneath bone bed,
Turner's bonk. *This track*
ay fer tackle trapesers
an sedge seekers. 'Ere
yo' need geopatience ...

... *'Ere's the fault.*

.
.
.

A boundary fault
in boundaryless leys –
The Straits am Cotwall End's release.
Tek the warty newts
pooled up theya: hondstonding
to tailwave, each egg leafwrapped,
larvae trans to efts trans to titan
since eocene.

Tek track
ovaled through 'awthorn

to heath, wood, grassland –
brooke, pool then spring.
Yo' wonder wheya yo' am:
protolith lost in foliation.

Petrologic Cinquain .4

Mudrock,
kinetic rains
segment the shale and silt;
an overlooked fissility –
Time traps.

Keeper of Geology

Pedestrians pass Graham,
unblinking in stone
stepped strides – Anagogical
gaze, calm smile.
With pushchairs armed
with market loot, taking
rest at Duncan Edwards' feet,
he works down Broadway,
pocket readied with loupe,
field notes, clinometer.
Graham hears the sounds under Dudley:

seven
legged wyvern
props our streets
with upturned feet –
300 tonne foundations
harmonised from Wenlock,
guards thin grain preservation
of Silurian soft tissues (Graham
says, *iss geology's Holy Grail)*, sirens
passengers through cathedral arch – portals –
to Little Tess, Hurst, Singing Cavern. Float
slow and mute, keep it on its back, spy
aragonite vaults that gape and bear
Castle Hill. Graham cuts Tipton
Road, taps toe every few
feet, listening for
echoes under
tarmac.

Slow Build/Burn

Magenta calcite drips:
Earth's slow seeping
into horned comber
colonises bluebrick
tunnels and adits.
We shed skins quicker
than this leaden lag
rebuilding. Like
wet-the-beds and poppies
popping through the hulk
husks of Crystal Mile,
still stained by saltpetre,
potash, red lead oxides.
Or the inward orbit fall
of Roundoak, Merry Hill,
whatever next. Whatever next?

Errare

They know their address, they don't know where they are.
Kenneth White

West Park wanderer,
erratic and stiff,
exforms in shades
cast over pathways:
Eros pole, glacially
guided from Arenig –
an arrow rebinding space.

Fred and Ken err perma-trias
tracks, check the state of chestnuts
and their own scape. *Iss too icy still,
ay it, me mon. Them ay ripe.* Shrug.

On to bowling green
and their own Aegil,
but never without a slight
palm pat against wet Felsite –
cosmos-pointing and terrafirmed,
enforming in firm attention –
a honing farewell.

Where Water Runs

When your name is mentioned on earth
for the final time; your final death,
chain coral cordoned wyvern still
squats below street level, almost immobile –
parastichy curled – spine arched watershed
conducting runoff. Flow east, over frustules,
nudibranch, kelp to Trent, Humber, Spurn Point.
Flow west, through fenestrida fiefdoms to Stour,
Severn, Mor Hafren. The ken of your kin cor
count the back and forth of these loops. Onuma
lost in the slow simple shredding of water through rock.

The Cutting

Rusted hummock of rusted sands,
torrid tanned cobbles, ovalled,
watch numb graves watching back
at wagging boys scaling stacks
of morainic concretions
left from slow floes.
Roots tentacle lamina grounds,
rope swing noosed over boss' frown
initiates these ephebes, taking
turns through covet, making
brave leaps as grinning clan
stand with stones, marksman
each oscillating rite. In quarries
boys bioturbate to burtite.

The Cutting #2

Sephardim boys shadow
BMXs behind business-park rails,
search Hayes Cutting in dayra drifts
for edge-base away from mom's gaze.

Corrugated iron, tipped tyres, chipped
bricks form dens on basal beds. Nearly
teen Safina etched into dusty anticline
with the sharp end of rusted fails.

Wargames of pebble shots at tramps' tinnies
punctuate trials with dad's superkings
then top trumps, then bush porn. This dipping
sequence holds placoderm, polypterid, actinopteri

and youthful peregrinations, grinding against ghost lineage.

9.

"Wings are a constraint that makes it possible to fly."[96]

The title of this entry is taken from Canadian Poet, Robert Bringhurst's *The Tree of Meaning*, a collection of lectures that fuse myth, folklore, language and politics with ecological perspective. In this quotation, he considers the magic and beauty that can be found or achieved in formal restriction and the intrinsic constraints of the natural realm.

In her preface to *Geopoetics in Practice* Hawkins says, Resonating with growing attention to embodiment and affect, geopoetics seems to me to be important in a recent reshaping not only of geographic expression but also of how geographic writers approach the space of the page, where composition as well as content becomes a geographic practice'.[97]

I've always found that formalist verse offers this. There is an untranslatable power in the act of placing poetic restriction on one's work. Forcing the mind to think in, not just sound, image, mood and theme, but in rhythm, rhyme and meter, brings about new ways of arranging thoughts and perceiving things. One finds sonic and thematic links, clashes and connections

---

[96] Bringhurst, R., *The Tree of Meaning: Thirteen Talks* (Counterpoint, California: 2007)

[97] Hawkins, H 'Preface' to *Geopoetics in Practice* (New York: Routledge, 2020) xii

between words and phrases, moods and themes, that would have been unnoticed without the attention to form. It is, as Bringhurst states, the necessary restriction that allows for things to take off. To transcend, as birds do, the different and divergent terrains of earth, air and water. This is a noble goal for the poet – to produce work which can act efficiently and effectively in different terrains – ecological, social, philosophical and spiritual. A Blakean Fourfold Vision perhaps?! Poetry is concerned with the multi-layered, intermixed terrains.

My work as poet in residence for the Black Country Geological Society is bound up in exploring the natural and earthy; in noticing its fearful symmetries. Geological observations of the world are also focused on pattern or structure, and on controlled investigation, extrapolation and portrayal. As such, not experimenting with form would be neglectful to the traditions of geopoetics, to the structures of the region's stratigraphy, as well as the patterns in ecology and place-identity evident in the Black Country Geopark. As I go about my drifts through the geosites there is a sense of attempting to dig into the grounds – literally and symbolically – this became a formal feature of my poems too. I'm investigating the links between landscape, community and individuals, and in doing so, am navigating down to a base layer. A rock solid platform that allows for poetic observations akin to Bringhurst's bird symbol. Here, I am trapped below the surface, on the immovable bedrock of our disparate topographies. Down here, I see things swarm, flood out in rhizomes. Down here, I see this swarming in rhythmite regularity.

A form that does justice to this is the American Imagist Cinquain; a short five-line poem tied together in strict syllabic measurements. Each line gets longer as the poem descends earthwards, allowing for slow, methodical meditation and magnification. It then hits its poetic bedrock with a snappy return to the thematic and formal aspect the poet began line one with – resulting in a sense of getting to the bottom of the thing, and yet returning too. In my adaptation of the form, called the Petrologic Cinquain, I use this shaping and sounding to delve into the makeup of the rocks and the conditions from which they form. It magnifies as the poem descends, like a petrologist's microscope would. It cuts the formations and slices the sections with its line breaks and enjambments in the way this field of geology divides rock types and gazes at thin sections of time and matter.

In *New Poetries* Aaron Kunin states, 'placing a limit on one area of decision making encourages surprising inventions in other areas'.[98] Using only the absolutely necessary words and totally accurate combinations of words – in terms of rhythm and rhyme – yields an almost alchemical result; accidental thematic conjugations, solutions and juxtapositions. This alchemy comes from the etymological roots of words that look and sound alike as well as the accidental happening upon a new thought from one totally different. W. N. Herbert comments on this, stating, 'Poetry is a means whereby we can discover what we didn't know we knew. Form is a means of generating these unknown messages... Chaos can be contained within an underlying and finally affirmative order'.[99] We're back with Eliot's scientific solution and the geopoetic preoccupation of seeking new modes of expression (logos) from contact with the 'chaos-mos'.

Form works in relation to how one experiences things too; how the infinite and infinitesimal share spaces, how a small observation or sense can lead to a multitude of memories, desires, regressions etc. and most importantly in the ways geology and the lay of the land might find form. This has much in common with Levertov's ideas of Organic Form. She suggests two routes, 'the idea that content, reality, experience,

---

[98] Aaron Kunin, *New Poetries*, From, *The Handbook of creative Writing*, 213
[99] W. N. Herbert, *What is Form*, From, *The Handbook of creative Writing*, 204

is essentially fluid and must be given form' and 'this sense of seeking out inherent, though not immediately apparent form'. She argues that 'it is a method of apperception [...] based on an intuition of an order, a form beyond forms, in which partake, and of which man's creative works are analogies, resemblances, natural allegories'.[100] In my poems, I'm attempting to express the apprehension of deep time and geological wonder, and the ways in which these things and movements branch out into community, culture and place-identity. These poems are Graptolites in their shifts. In measuring my verses with attention to the nature of this rhizomatic observation and geological unearthing, 'content and form are in a state of dynamic interaction'.[101]

The Heroic Couplet, and the Sonnet offer further form and shape to the geological focus of this collection. The strict iambic metre and rhyming couplets of Heroic Verse are associated with epic narratives and drama. Each couplet forming a distinct rhetorical and metrical unit, adding line / layer by line / layer to the overall expression. Sound, shape and rhythm pushing forward and pulling back, bearing against that which precedes and follows. The Heroic Couplet is a stratigraphic and

---

[100] Levertov, D., *Some Notes on Organic Form*, From *New and selected Essays*, rwwsoundings.com, 1-2

[101] Levertov, 1-2

rhythmite form. The shape and pace of the sonnet is similarly cathedral-esque. Its dividing quatrains, octaves, sestets and couplets arch, perfect in symmetry, forming on further arches, aiming to the transcendent and rooted in the ground.

Finding the right word / form is a poet's masochistic pleasure and raison d'etre. Re-finding the right word/form (logos) is the geopoet's. In form, the geopoet seeks a "model that transcends the entropic dimensions of customary exoticizing manoeuvres whilst at the same time presenting new configurations of place, language and self".[102] In my work, I've experimented with forms that express and illuminate the sounds, rhythms and shapes of the landscape and their inherent geological features; in formalist Latin and Japanese structures, in reimagined concrete poems (See *Foram* and *Pizza Fossil*), and in Levertov's Organic Verse these are expressions of geological method and observation as a route to conveying that grounded sense of world. This is akin to White's practice as poet, essayist and way writer - these three creative and scholarly pursuits fuse, form bridges and create a new geopoetic form: "the general pattern is archipelago-like, as the text is made up of a series of numbered, apparently unrelated fragments, sometimes

---

[102] Fordick, C., 'Kenneth White and Victor Segalen' from *Grounding a World: Essays on the Work of Kenneth White*, eds Bowd, G., Forsdick, C., Bissell, N., (Alba Editions: 2005) p.149

including just one or two sentences".[103] Tim Cresswell draws on the fragmentary and difficult to map, saying he wants to 'gesture towards the possibilities of a promiscuous version of hybrid geopoetics' creating something 'hybrid in intent and form'.[104] Cresswell argues that this playfulness, archipelago - likeness and hybridity 'challenge the conventions of both 'poetry' and 'academic writing', and it is in this hybridity that I see an emergent 'geopoetics' that provides new opportunities to grasp the hyperobject of climate change as well as other similarly ungraspable things'.[105]

In thinking of the right word / form for her stones, Hallett realises that "Stones are a gestural language / A language without words / like music",[106] as such, the expression and the form that this takes must be gestural too – it must meet that geopoetic crossing-point-target of intellect and instinct, being and earth.

This links nicely with David Constantine's arguments:

---

[103] Bsaithi, O., 'In Arab Lands: A Geopoetic Sketch', *Grounding a World: Essays on the Work of Kenneth White*, eds Bowd, G., Forsdick, C., Bissell, N., (Alba Editions: 2005) p. 163

[104] Cresswell T. Beyond geopoetics: For hybrid texts. Dialogues in Human Geography. 2021;11(1):36-39. doi:10.1177/2043820620986399

[105] ibid

[106] Hallett, p.39

> Poetry is common. The stuff of it is common, even commonplace. Poetry comes from what we as human beings have in common. It puts us in touch with our shared realities ... poetry helps us realise common things better. [However] poetic language has to be other and peculiar. If the poetic line comes so close to the spoken and written sentences of everyday that it merges with them, it will lose its purchase on the realities of everyday.[107]

Constantine's version of poetry is an uncanny mode of language – both familiar and unfamiliar. Combining different types of language or vernacular – the everyday, dialect, scientific – helps to root my pieces in a particular thinking – a Black Country Geopoetic – making the overall collection both Common and Peculiar, This creates a queer stew of different voices or discourses, different places, different realities. The common and peculiar, like flow and friction, give each other purchase and allow things to be grounded.

Brendan Kennelly adds to this in his thoughts about outsider voices:

> poetry is both a continuing revolution and ultimate democracy because it is both questioning these voices [...] and also creating for them the kind of space which may become the overview of the inherited values of

[107] David Constantine, 'Common and Peculiar', in *Strong Words: Modern Poets on Modern Poetry*, Ed W.N. Herbert and Matthew Hollis. (Newcastle Upon Tyne: Bloodaxe. 2000) pp. 226 - 227

> the poet-questioner [...] surrendering to an outcast
> voice means that one surrenders to complexities of
> history, religion, geography, memory, language,
> family.[108]

The voices of my text are all 'outsider voices'. These outsiders
are given their place in speaker's corner, without interruption,
to make their accounts in critically, emotionally, passionately
informed tongues. As such, it has the potential to be that very
space of 'continuing revolution and ultimate democracy'. These
outsider voices are also the voices of the land - the lost songs
and stories of the earth, the messages we forgot how to read.

Hugh MacDiarmid, a poet of the rocks and of geology, says 'A
living dog is worth more than any number of dead lions.'
MacDiarmid suggests that the use of outsider voices and
disrupting traditional modes of expression has political and / or
spiritual emancipatory power. He calls the resource 'an
inexhaustible quarry of subtle and significant sound'.

This is a geopoetic trajectory – one of uncovering and
reconnecting, of finding what might be within the known, of
grounding oneself in the previously unnoticed and gaining a
deeper understanding of one's locale, land, world. As Sarah De

[108] Brendan Kennelly, 'Voices', in *Strong Words: Modern Poets on
Modern Poetry*, Ed W.N. Herbert and Matthew Hollis. (Newcastle
Upon Tyne: Bloodaxe, 2000) pp. 213 - 214

Leeuw suggests, 'This act of locating is central to being a poet, an essayist, and a geographer – it's a crucial part of how I think and write about geopoetics'.[109] We're in the abyss and it feels like home.

[109] De Leeuw, S, 'Introduction' from *Geopoetics in Practice* (New York: Routledge, 2020) 6

Spring Heeled Jack

"First a young girl, then a man, felt a hand on their
shoulder, and turned to see the infernal one with
glowing face, bidding them a good evening."
Birmingham Post, September 1886

Coiled Tatzlwurm,
patient in dried hydrosphere –
inertia writhing
in lands of ore and cutting,
eyes gleaming, setting to spring.

Oilskinned Stollwurm,
forged in fortean faultlines,
old hags the bedrock.
Spring-pinned mare – this stollenwurm
jacks the slack pace of our streets.

Lindworm

Lindworm under Leasowes
muddied brooke bank, tracking
tended greens and walkways;
Shenstone etched in delicate circuit
where flow, rush, plunge quilts
slow steps passed urn, bench, footbridge:
Soft drone of petrichor.

In calm it makes its goblin market,
unnoticed, unheard. Set in vermi-
oubliettes as Halesowen bypasses
flood engines on routes to Brum.
Their own flow, rush, plunge. *They
used to come 'ere, but they doh come
'ere no more.* Lindworm under Leasowes
leaks its mulching bites under A458, no.9,
Whittington Road and Hawne Basin...

...turning scoop wheel under lapal tunnel
its half-sleep churning grumble-growls
in Murder Ballad rhythm out to Dudley
and the leisure steps of Leasowes' ramblers
feel skinshedding of lindworm mercy.

Petrologic Cinquain .5

Fireclay,
seat stone saggars
set on Brierley Bonk,
one thousand five hundred degrees –
lehred.

Stand Still

She slips shoes off. Soles into mudded soils:
Ironstone, Borax, Graphite, Pigiron
Olivine, limestone, Pyrolusite,
under cold teal skies and
the slow precipitation
of crisp oak leaves,
she is rained.

Bibble #3

She said, *iss just a rock,*
and she was right. *Yo'm
right, me wench,
an' thass the rub,
iss just a rock, beginning
as mixed minerals moulded,
filtered, crushed in crust plates
along the axis formin' leaves
'a foliation.* He has dirt under
her nails, tracing the variscan
fractals of spacetime fabric.

Ichthyolith

Bleached lichen webs the blushed sandstone
and mosses crawl and rasp roots roam
and silvered birch mudlarks its leaves
where umber-tan Stour waters weave,

and Matt skulks down the cut's tow path
somnambulist arm becomes a snath,
and scratches nails against the grains,
passing daily, left arm cranes

the Triassic interglacial lodes,
and watch the players dominoed
and sup in the Royal Exchange:
talons gritted in glassmaker range

of sediments – dark amber like his ale,
Matt sits and marks his nails,
unaware of dead etiolated teeth
of time clammed ichthyolith.

Fish rock gemmed in keratin
He touches it. It touches him.

Coccolithophore

In chain coral codas, she crystalised
convex plates with polysaccharides.
Her fearless radial symmetries
burn bright in sheer geometries:
raise white cliffs in pelagite spew;
colours the reef and mesh of foods;
cleans solutes with light. Gasses the wreck
in choral Ashet arabesques.

Father / Daughter bring tip to tongue
from another humanless and long
fieldwork drift to Shire Oak barr
tasting salt-driven wyvern's scar.

Call her Emiliani, Huxley, Coccolithophore.
Nothing so huge has ever been so small.

Foram

Float

    find form

        Fixed cell feeding nanonetworks: Springing
        pseudopodial netting to move, to ingest, to transfer.

        Unicellular beams in sympathetic constellations –
        a star, bristled singularity in worm hole – the w/hole
        bearers –

            Protist, phytoplankton, algae

                Twist-shell of agglutinated place-
                identity

                    So, it like, takes bits 'a sediment
                    from the sea an' brings it into isself
                    an' covers isself in cavities tharrare,
                    like, fixed, cemented by iss own
                    albumen. An' we were all like, wow,
                    like thass sorta like that feeling yo'
                    get when yo' come home, ay it? Iss
                    like a patchwork blanket: a cuirass.

                hang,
                    hew

        We are here still…
        …eukaryotic.

Petrologic Cinquain .6

Greywacke,
recrystallised
feldspathic slates, lithic
gneiss – fetal bab conglomerate –
Meshings.

On the Currents of Carbon Dioxide in Underground Caves

Cave mouths. Epikarst pores.
Where speleothem tines track the gas
of limestone regulations and ground air.
Breathes in rhythms, that wave in bands
of calcite tears. Seasons fluctuate
the heat, the air. In spring, c02 swings.
There's distinct atmospheres down here.

She points it out, little girl found,
in her wor(l)d grounding:
the strange fog of stoned exhales
misting like the roots of alien triffids
up to our human habitats.   Sitting.

Fossil Pizza

Left on steps leading
up
Marsh Pit
hundreds of prints
ignored
in Winter's wetness.

```
Symphyla
T
bRyozoa
   O        ectoprocta
    M        y  e
    A        s  n
    Tunicate t  t
     O        o e
     P        i c
     Ostracod o
      Rugosa  p        b
      O       t        l
    z  I      e      phacop
 conoDont     r        s
   o  E       u        t
   i  A    straight horn
    diplopoda          i
                       d
```

She spies and plucks
it from the grit.
In small unweathered
palm, examining
Silurian seas:
eyes whitened
in Gwenved

115

10.

Geology puts you in touch with the earth and the space-time which is as old as she is. This provides embodied wayfinding wisdom of our locale, and re-opens a primeval, animal consciousness and self-awareness. Like the ancestral genius loci present in the rocks and soils, the ancestral beasts woken within us in our new wayfinding say; I am in all.

Wyvern

I knew the storm was gerrin closer. Thass what the bell pits tode
us. Over their cusps an' into the rut. Breathe slow. Tek quiet
steps. Yo'd spied the strange patterns peerin' back at yo'. An'
yo' come out soiled by iss tredin'. As yo' tred it treds into yo'.
They used to come 'ere but they doh come 'ere no more.
Weem touched by it somehow. Wyvern-swayed in the wild
roots woven round slag, pit bonk an' quarry. We see. We
know wass watchin'. Ready to rise. The Wrenna ripple beds
am sinuous, catenary marks 'a fleetin' move/moments, spellin'
out iss name:

WyvernWyvernWyvernWyvernWyvernWyvernWyvernWyv
ernWyvernWyvernWyven

Ruined cluniac bricks, municipal toilet an' playground - still,
silent, sedated. Edge, hedge, saplings an' teen-oaks – idle
railway laminae. Cooper's Bonk an' Snetter estates – just
hush and hushing. The almost silent hush from chain coral's
infinite coda. *I see the storm is gerrin closer.*
The moment moved into Alice-Time. Entering / re-entering.
Some paths ay med for mon. Some ay med by mon. Yo' scaled
em anyroad, day yo'?

About the Author

R. M. Francis is a lecturer in Creative and Professional Writing at the University of Wolverhampton. He's the author of two novels, *Bella* and *The Wrenna*, published with Wild Pressed Books, and a poetry collection, *Subsidence*, with Smokestack Books. In 2019 he was the inaugural David Bradshaw Writer in Residence at the University of Oxford and is currently Poet in Residence for The Black Country Geological Society. His academic research focuses on place-identity in the Black Country and has been published in a number of edited collections; he co-edited the book, *Smell, Memory and Literature in the Black Country* (Palgrave McMillan).

Acknowledgements

Thanks go to the editors of the following, where earlier versions of the work and some of the poems first found a home: *Earth Lines: Geopoetry and Geopoetics; Microtravel: Confinement, Deceleration, Microspection; Osmosis Press; Elsewhere Journal; Seek Poetry; Under the Radar.* I'm indebted to the work of the Black Country Geological Society, Scottish Centre for Geopoetics and the International Institute for Geopoetics. Special thanks to Patrick Corbett, Norman Bissell, Tim Cresswell, Kenneth White, Alyson Hallett, Harry Gallagher, Ben Colbert, Lee Armstrong, Liz Berry, Roy MacFarlane and Emma Purshouse, whose wild conversations and poetry helped shape this project. This research was funded and enabled by the University of Wolverhampton's Doctoral College Early Research Award Scheme.